A SHORT PRIMER
FOR PROTESTANTS

AN ABRIDGEMENT OF HIS

FULL LENGTH HADDAM HOUSE BOOK

A SHORT
PRIMER FOR
PROTESTANTS

JAMES HASTINGS NICHOLS

Association Press · *New York*

A SHORT PRIMER FOR PROTESTANTS

———

Copyright © 1957 by
National Board of Young Men's Christian Associations

———

Association Press, 291 Broadway, New York 7, N. Y.

Price, 50 cents

Library of Congress catalog card number: 57-5492

 475

Printed in the United States of America

CONTENTS

A SHORT PRIMER

FOR PROTESTANTS

CHAPTER ONE

Protestants and Other Christians

THE DEFINITION OF PROTESTANTISM presents two sides. The actual Protestant churches that we know came into existence, for the most part, in the period of the Reformation, the sixteenth and seventeenth centuries. They organized as separate churches in a mood of complete disillusionment with the existing Roman Catholic church organization. And there remains in Protestantism this memory of a solemn repudiation, of death and rebirth. One important half of the truth, consequently, locates the origins of Protestantism in the Reformation, and defines it by contrast to Roman Catholicism. As Bishop Dun puts it, all Christians are naturally Catholic until they learn by bitter experience to be something better. And the commonest meaning of the word "Protestant" today in Western countries is simply, "any Christian who denies the authority of the Roman pope."

But if only this half of the truth is seen, Protestantism is quite misconceived. To the taunt, "Where was your church before the Reformation?" an Anglican replied shrewdly if somewhat inelegantly, "Where was your face before you washed it this morning?" Protestantism also represents a genuine revival of the life and gospel of the apostles, and even a continuation of certain major streams of religious life of the Latin middle ages. On several important issues Protestantism is in the main line of Western Christian history and it is modern Romanism which represents the innovation and "protest." Modern Roman Catholicism was radically reorganized in creed, government, and worship in reaction to the Reformation, and is historically incomprehensible save as a protest against Protestantism. Many peripheral aspects of the life of the undivided church which the Reformation had attacked or belittled were now deliberately moved into the center of emphasis and many novelties established. A new denomination was created, as "Protestant" in the negative sense as Lutheranism or Calvinism, and yet like them having also certain roots and precedents in the undivided church. Modern Romanism and modern Protestantism alike are partly revolutionary and partly traditional and neither can be fully understood without relating it to the other.

The Reformation

When the Reformation came in that wonderful generation in the second quarter of the sixteenth century it burst forth almost simultaneously over most of Latin Christendom from the suppressed aspirations of centuries. Its leaders were all trained as Catholics and most of them had been ordained Catholic priests. Its most effective propagandists were simple clergy all over Europe who now found courage to say what had long lain on their consciences. Most of them had no intention of leaving the church of their fathers; they wished to reform it. These were no wanton revolutionaries. Luther himself had remained a submissive churchman and exemplary monk, vicar of eight monasteries, for ten years after he had discovered the meaning of evangelical reconciliation with God. He only discovered and defended the original conciliarist organization of the church after he had

11

been shocked to find that the papal monarchy stood pat on outrageous corruption and thus raised in his mind the problem of its credentials.

Luther, as a parish pastor, found that his people were being told that they could buy for cash immunity from the due consequences of sin. As the Catholic princes wrote the pope five years after Luther posted his theses, "License to sin with impunity is granted for money. . . . Hence come fornications, adulteries, incests, perjuries, homicides, thefts, and a whole hydra of evil." Luther had questioned the whole assumption that men could profit by the ministry of the saints, not by accepting the fellowship of their crosses, but simply by a cash payment at the grilled window of the Treasury of Merits on the Tiber. He denied that the papal court had ever possessed the power to release men from punishment, and asked the embarrassing question, supposing that the pope has such power, "Why doesn't he empty purgatory for the sake of the most holy charity" rather than doing it only partially and only for money?

Only gradually did Luther perceive how this blasphemous conception that priests were able to manipulate the Almighty by incantations, formulas, and liturgical transactions had pervaded the whole sacramental system of the church. Private masses, for example, were widely performed on the assurance that God could so be put under obligation to perform whatever services the purchaser of the masses had in mind. This was ordinary pagan conjuring and magic. Was this the living God who could be summoned into a wafer like a djinn from the *Arabian Nights* and then sent on errands, or constrained to moderate his judgments of sinners by the assurance of a priest that certain financial adjustments had been made? Was there really any man on earth with the power, in order to put pressure on wayward rulers, to enjoin God from his eternal purpose of reconciliation in their territories? But when Luther and the Catholic princes addressed remonstrances to the papal court they looked to the wrong quarters. That court set up a Commission of Cardinals to study the problem of reform, but when the prelates submitted their report in 1537, it contained among many damaging revelations the significant observation that the source of all this corruption was the

13

absolute dominion of the Pope. The report was suppressed and the Roman Gestapo, the Inquisition, was revived. Truly the Reformation had not come too soon. It was time that those who believed in the Reign of God in Christ should re-examine the Roman title to authority in the church.

The Roman Church Today

That time is not yet over. To this day the Roman church has never been able to keep itself free from spiritual and moral rottenness except in the presence of criticism from without. Consolidated into a new sect at the Council of Trent, on principles we must presently examine, Romanism has remained a caricature of the gospel in the lands of the Mediterranean and Latin America where it has been freed of criticism by Inquisition and censorship. Roman Catholics admit that their communion is at its best in Protestant countries, Germany, England, Holland, the United States, or where, as in France, the majority of the nation have declared their emancipation. For the sake of vigorous and spiritual Romanism, the Protestant

14

church remains today as necessary as at the Reformation. Modern Romanism cannot live of its own resources. The road of spiritual despotism leads eternally to corruption save when confronted by the force of moral example from without. Thus the evangelical witness of Protestantism has made it possible for millions of evangelical Christians to live and die with only passing discomfort within the Roman church without becoming Protestants themselves. A Romanism which has repudiated the ancient conciliarist* principle is ever afterward dependent for its religious integrity on a sister Protestantism.

Protestants who search their own history, however, will recognize the pains of readjustment and the temptations to which Romanism has succumbed only more completely than Protestantism. Protestants, also, as we are to show in the following chapters, have again and again yielded to the temptation to set up false securities, to seek salva-

---

* The terms conciliarist and conciliar as used in this book refer to a type of church government by representative assemblies or councils, in contrast to a monarchical or absolutist pattern. See p. 87 f.

tion in institutional loyalties, moralism, creedal orthodoxies, or Biblical literalism, all substitutes for the personal trust in the living God and the acceptance of his free grace taught by the evangel. Not seldom in the course of its history, moreover, has Protestantism had occasion to be grateful for the Roman church. At the least, God has granted us hundreds and thousands of true lovers of Christ in the Roman communion who have been his ministers by their lives or writings to Protestants. The international organization of Romanism, again, has repeatedly been a reminder to Protestants that their loyalties ought not to be merely provincial. And by its very external rigidity Romanism, however indirectly, has served to remind many subjectivistic and humanistic Protestants of the objectivity and the superhuman authority of the Christian revelation. Perhaps the God who brings into existence that which does not exist, intends some new thing out of the complementary and mutually strengthening witnessing of the sister communions of the West.

The Orthodox Churches

There remains nearly one third of Christendom organized in the churches who proudly call themselves "Orthodox." The most powerful and important of the sections of Eastern Orthodoxy today is, of course, the Russian Orthodox Church. With it may be grouped, however, some twenty churches of a similar type, chiefly located in the Balkans and the Near East. All together they represent nearly a third of all Christians, and a third type of Christianity which is neither Protestant nor Roman Catholic, but antedates both in its unbroken continuity from the fourth and fifth centuries. Some understanding of Eastern Orthodoxy is thus important as providing another perspective on the character of evangelical Protestantism, as well as for pressing practical questions which arise from the relationship of Orthodox Catholics to evangelicals both in the World Council of Churches and in the National Council of Churches in the United States.

With regard to the definition of the Christian gospel, however, evangelicals and Orthodox Catholics find themselves in some tension. It is the boast of Orthodoxy that it adheres to the doctrinal decisions of the early councils of the church, especially those of the fourth and fifth centuries, every jot and tittle, without any such amendments or modifications as have since been introduced both by Romanists and by Protestants. For Orthodoxy, consequently, the doctrine of Christianity has been stated finally and irrevocably in the language and philosophical concepts of the creeds of the fourth and fifth centuries, and it is neither to be added to nor reinterpreted in the terms of other cultural situations. The "Nicene" Creed and the formula of Chalcedon state for all eternity what a Christian believes and how he conceives that belief. While a majority of evangelicals have probably always been willing to subscribe to these creeds, they have never accepted them as final or infallible. The creeds are authoritative for evangelicals, but only because and in so far as they adequately indicate the gospel message. And that Word of God must be freshly heard and interpreted in every situation. Orthodox Catholicism thus presents a static traditionalism in contrast to the dynamic evangelical conception of the church.

The Misuse of Terms

There is no use arguing over words, and life is too short to campaign against incorrect usage. A word of regret may be expressed, nevertheless, at that partiality of popular usage which has accorded in the modern English-speaking world the grand old word "Catholic"—universal—to the Roman communion, while to that great company stemming institutionally from the Reformation it attaches the term "Protestant." The emptiness of the term "Protestant" is in large measure the outcome of a curious inversion of the meaning of the word "protest" since Elizabethan days. "Protestant" to Elizabethan Englishmen did not signify an objector, but rather one who bore a witness, who made an avowal. The contemporary "Confessing Church" of the German resistance has caught again the original significance of "Protestantism" in the English-speaking world, as a testifying church, a witnessing church. This was the connotation which made suitable the adoption of the term "Protestant." Only after the word "protest" changed its emphasis from the positive to the negative sense in general use did the term "Protestant" come to include all dissent from Romanism, whatever its positive avowal.

Outside English-speaking lands the sons of the Reformation have not been betrayed in this way by the natural evolution of language. On the Continent and in Latin America the terms "evangelicals" or "reformed" are generally used, the one sometimes applied more particularly to the Lutheran and the other to the Calvinist wings of the Reformation tradition. Neither term, with all the special connotations it may have acquired, suffers from such serious disadvantages as a title for the sum-product of the Reformation as does the word now irretrievably established in English usage and in general misunderstanding. "Evangelicalism" expresses best the positive message to which early "Protestants" were witnessing, the good news of healing in Christ's kingdom. A less ambiguous title for this book would thus be "a primer of evangelical Christianity," and when the word Protestant is used, it signifies, not everything non-

Roman and non-Eastern Orthodox, but *evangelical* Protestantism, the Protestantism born of and living by a witness to the full and revivified gospel.

We shall begin with a survey of the evangelical fellowship and proceed to a definition of certain principles of Protestant life and thought. In this statement of evangelical faith, as with all Protestant statements, we shall be testifying to the experience of the fellowship, in this case of many living and many dead, but with no notion of finality or adequacy. This statement lies under the correction of the unending dialogue of the evangelical community with the God who makes himself known there, and will have served its purpose if it brings someone into that fellowship and to the hearing of the speaking God.

21

CHAPTER TWO

The Protestant Movement

THE MOST FAMILIAR THEME of critics of Protestantism is its divisiveness. Each succeeding religious census in the United States turns up a few more startlingly named "store-front churches." We are now about the three hundred mark, and old Bossuet's theme of the infinite divisiveness of Protestantism seems amply justified by its ongoing history.

Unity and Diversity

Yet we should not be hasty. It will enable us to keep some hold on reality to remember that 90 per cent of the church members of America are found within twenty denominations, and over 80 per cent within thirteen denominations.

We may even be permitted a further reduction; more than four out of five American Protestants belong to one of the six great families of Protestant

22

churches: Baptist and Disciples, Methodist, Lutheran, Anglican and Episcopalian, Presbyterian and Reformed, Congregational-Christian. These same six families include nine-tenths of the Protestants in the rest of the world. We do not mean to underrate the richness and variety of Protestantism, nor the full claim of smaller groups to the name of evangelical Protestantism, nor the fact that there is not nearly enough co-operation and consolidation within Protestantism. These things are all important truths. What is not sufficiently recognized, however, is the fact that behind the perennially prolific frontier of organizational Protestantism, the main body has displayed a remarkable institutional stability.

Far more important than numerical considerations in these matters is the inner meaning of this complicated organization of Protestantism. Romanists often criticize Protestant divisions with the too hasty assumption that Protestant denominations are all sects in the sense that Roman Catholicism is a sect. This is, on the whole, not true. One can find Protestant denominations who maintain, like Rome, that they alone are the true church. Certain

Lutheran, Baptist, and "holiness" groups come to mind. For the great majority of Protestants, however, the denominational structure is only an administrative differentiation within a common faith. Methodists, Presbyterians, Congregationalists, for example, who have actually united in Canada, generally regard each other as equally Christian, and their rivalry is no more serious than that between Jesuits and Dominicans, Benedictines and Redemptorists, Irish Catholics and German Catholics, the followers of Maritain and Sturzo, and the supporters of Franco and the Inquisition. The Roman Catholics have a central agency which can at least force silence when the dissensions of various Romanist traditions or national organizations become too hot, but one may seriously doubt whether the suspension of central discipline would disclose one degree more of real trust and fellowship within the Roman communion than exists within Protestantism. The difference between the two great communions is that Protestants wash their dirty linen in public. The method leads to greater scandal and inefficiency, but avoids, on the other hand, the in-

24

trigue, tattle-telling and hypocrisy which corrode the relationships of Roman Catholics.

But uniformity has been an ideal of much of Protestantism for much of its history. This conception, in fact, provides us with the most convenient key to the confusing history of Protestant institutions. The movements of the Reformation may be divided into two groups, a conservative group which retained the medieval conception of a uniform, church-dominated state and culture, and a liberal wing, often persecuted, which continued rather the medieval traditions of separatist congregational life or of individualist humanists or mystics. The former group produced the three great ecclesiastical systems of the sixteenth and seventeenth centuries, the Lutheran state-churches of Germany and Scandinavia, the Anglican church, and the Reformed churches of Switzerland, Holland, France, Scotland, and New England. Together with the new Romanism of Spain, Italy, France, and east-central Europe these three great ecclesiastical cultures constituted a renewal of the medieval ideal for two centuries, as it were, four medievalisms living side by side, in debate and often in war. All claimed to rest on the dogmatic tradition of the ancient church and all rejected Copernicus and Galileo. All rejected also, with even greater severity than had the later middle ages, the religious groups which gave up the ideal of uniformity. Romanists, Calvinists, Lutherans, Anglicans found an ominous convergence of purpose in the savage persecution of separatist sects and rationalistic and mystical individualists, the humanistic and "Anabaptist" movements. We may thus distinguish three varieties of authoritarian Protestantism and two general tendencies of a non-authoritarian Protestantism in the first two centuries of our history.

The end of the seventeenth century, however, marked a tremendous revolution in the relation of European culture and states to Christianity. The savage and sterile wars of religion in France, Holland, Germany, England, and Scotland convinced the groups directing these states that the authoritarian, religiously uniform society was no longer possible. Roman Catholicism has never accepted this judgment of history as final and still dreams of a "Roman Catholic state," even for the United

States of America. All of the three great Protestant medievalisms, on the other hand, accepted the judgment, slowly, regretfully, imperfectly, but finally. And as the pressure of persecution eased, the two suppressed Protestant tendencies, the humanist and mystical, and the separatist congregationalists, enjoyed *their* Reformation. The triumph of this free Protestantism did not so much produce new denominations and movements, although some such appeared, like the Methodists, as it captured the thought and life of the formerly uniform churches. Humanist, rationalist, and mystical tendencies established themselves as important and sometimes dominant streams in the theology of Lutherans, Anglicans, and Calvinists in the eighteenth and nineteenth centuries. The Anabaptist conception of the separation of the church from the state profoundly changed the thinking even of churches which remained nominally state churches, while such churches experienced a penetration of voluntary fellowships of the Anabaptist type *within* their inherited structure.

One result has been that modern Lutherans and Presbyterians, for example, to say nothing of Anglicans, often find themselves more congenial to men like Erasmus or Servetus or Sebastian Franck than they do to those founders from whom they stem. As Harnack wrote of some of the Anabaptist leaders who were fiercely attacked by the great Reformers, "many of these noble and reverend characters come nearer to us than the figures of an heroic Luther and an iron Calvin." Thus the minor and suppressed strains of the Reformation have come to be those most characteristic of modern Protestantism. It is this internal revolution, together with ever-increasing mutual borrowings down the generations, and the common inheritance of evangelical Christianity down to the Reformation, that makes it possible and indeed necessary to treat Protestantism as a whole, even if a whole composed of diverse tendencies in continual tension and fruitful debate.

That branch of the faith which was, up to the end of the eighteenth century, almost entirely the religion of Northern and Western Europe, became, in four or five generations more, solidly rooted in every continent and major people. While still numbering less than half of all Christians, evangelical Protestantism has been steadily gaining in proportion to the two other branches of Christendom since the sixteenth century. And in these centuries it has made the greatest impact on the societies and cultures it has touched of all branches of the Church. The whole balance of Protestantism is shifting, with the Asiatic leadership rapidly occupying a full equality with the European and North American contingents, while the extraordinarily rapid growth of Protestantism in a country like Brazil points to major changes in Latin America. And what this will mean for the life and thought of the whole defies prediction.

Protestant Catholicity

The last generation or so has also seen a great revival of the Reformation and conciliar awareness of the visible church universal. This recovery has found institutional expression in the so-called "ecumenical" movement, an *evangelical* catholicism, now co-ordinated in the manifold activities of the World Council of Churches. To an historian of Christianity this institutional consolidation of Protestantism, and the rapprochement between

29

Protestantism and Orthodox Catholicism, is probably the most striking development of the first half of the twentieth century. At times it has seemed that this movement was an enthusiasm of the clergy alone, if not merely of ecclesiastical globe-trotters, but the Second World War proved it to be sustained by a deep and fresh awareness among the laity of the essential oneness of Christ's body everywhere, across all military and cultural frontiers. Just as the leaders of this movement were able to bring together representatives from the recently warring people after the First World War, and just as representatives of the Younger Churches actually at war were able to worship together at Madras, so in our day the fellowship and trust of Christians is almost the sole channel of healing among the shattered peoples of Europe. And in all the great assemblies of the church universal in the last generation, at Stockholm, Jerusalem, Lausanne, Oxford, Edinburgh, and Madras, the basis and reality of union was found, not in theological or ethical discussion, but in common adoration, in the memorable services of worship when the "communion of saints" became actuality.

Actual organic consolidation of Protestant denominations seems agonizingly protracted, yet over thirty mergers have been consummated in this generation. The most striking of these in America is the formation of the United Church of Canada of Methodist, Congregational, and Presbyterian churches, an institutional recognition of the essential unity of the Puritan group of denominations. The same groups are negotiating for similar ventures in other parts of the British Commonwealth of Nations and like possibilities have been discussed now and again in the United States.

Such institutional reform, however, advisable as much of it undoubtedly is, is not the most important aspect of the ecumenical recovery of the church universal. Neither international conferences nor the consolidation of denominational administration are worth the effort unless they contribute to the religious realization of the local congregation that it is simply the local representative of Christ's worldwide fellowship. Wherever that realization is strong enough to shake the patterns of class and national and racial pride in a community, there the ecumenical movement finds fulfillment,

31

whatever the administrative superstructure may be.

The present tendency is indicated by the transition Harry Emerson Fosdick describes from his earlier view that "we make the church" to his present conviction, "the church makes us." Out of this discussion, which will also be carried on across the Atlantic with European Protestantism and across the Pacific with the Younger Churches, may emerge a more comprehensive synthesis of the insights of the varied strands of the Reformation movement. The ecumenical rising may then see a new Protestantism.

Let us now turn from this outline of the Protestant movement with its internal tensions and varieties to a survey of those convictions and insights which have defined the common heritage.

CHAPTER THREE

The Sole Headship of Jesus Christ

VIEWING THE REFORMATION and the four succeeding Protestant centuries together, we may describe five enduring motifs of Protestant life and thought.

Christ's Intrinsic Authority

The fundamental principle of the Reformation is perhaps most eloquently stated by an Eastern Orthodox writer, Dostoievsky, in the words of his Grand Inquisitor, the voice of the Roman Counter-Reformation. The story, it will be recalled, is laid in Spain, in Seville, in the most terrible time of the Inquisition, when fires were lighted every day to the glory of God. And there in his infinite mercy Christ came down among men, down to the hot pavement of the southern town in which, on the

33

day before, almost a hundred heretics had *ad majorem gloriam Dei* been burnt by the cardinal, the Grand Inquisitor.* He was recognized by all and surrounded by worshipers and children crying "Hosanna," while the crowd wept and kissed the earth under his feet. The blind recovered their sight once more, and the dead were raised before all the people. And then, suddenly, came the guards of the Inquisition, who laid hands on him, and in death-like silence, led him away.

In the blackness of that night the cardinal visited Christ in his cell and rebuked him for daring to bring even there his gospel of evangelical freedom, promising to burn him the next day as the worst of heretics.

Thou didst desire man's free love, that he should follow thee freely, enticed and taken captive by thee. In place of the ancient rigid law, man must hereafter with free heart decide for himself what is good and what is evil, having only thy image before him as his guide. . . . Thou didst crave faith freely given, not based on miracle. Thou didst crave for free love and

* *The Brothers Karamazov,* Part II, Book V, Chapter V. From the edition by Crown Publishers, Inc., New York.

34

not the base raptures of the slave before the might that has overawed him for ever. . . . The freedom of their faith was dearer to thee than anything in those days fifteen hundred years ago.

How is the weak soul to blame that it is unable to receive such terrible gifts? And if for the sake of the bread of Heaven thousands and tens of thousands shall follow thee, what is to become of the millions and tens of thousands of millions of creatures who will not have the strength to forego the earthly bread for the sake of the heavenly? Canst thou have come simply to the elect and for the elect? But if so, it is a mystery and we cannot understand it. And if it is a mystery, we too have a right to preach a mystery, and to teach them that it's not the free judgment of their hearts, not love that matters, but a mystery which they must follow blindly even against their conscience. So we have done. We have corrected thy work and founded it upon *miracle, mystery,* and *authority.* We shall deceive them again, for we will not let thee come to us again. That deception will be our suffering, for we shall be forced to lie. Why hast thou come now to hinder us? And why dost thou look silently and searchingly at me with thy mild eyes? Be angry. I don't want thy love, for I love thee not.

We may be permitted to emphasize the issue of this dialogue between the voice of the Reformation and the voice of Tridentine Catholicism, even at the risk of pedantry. The Reformation rests simply on the figure of Christ as accessible to all men in the gospel, a Christ who needs no recommendations, no credentials, who can be trusted by the power of the Spirit to evoke recognition and the love of free men. This is not simply the "right of private judgment." Every man must, to be sure, even if in "great anxiety and terrible agony," make a free and responsible decision for himself. But it is God who entices and takes him captive in Christ, God in the figure of Christ, and God illumining the responsive mind and heart. "No man can say that Jesus is Lord but by the Holy Spirit." This is, if you will, the direct access of the believer to God, without patented ecclesiastical intermediaries, but it is no subjectivistic mysticism. This is a faith in the sufficient force of revelation in history, Jesus Christ, unique, indispensable, self-authenticating. The "elect" who receive such a "terrible" gift do always seem to be a minority among men. And the meaning of the incomplete lives of those tens of thousands of millions of creatures who do not receive this gift is indeed a mystery.

For all Protestants, the focus of God's Word, God's purpose and character, has always centered in Jesus Christ in his whole significance and in the context of history before and since. From this strange and partly alien prophet there come to us the unmistakable, authoritative tones of the eternal Christ of God. Our conception of the eternal Christ is thus indissolubly connected with the personality of the historical Jesus. And we have sufficient records of the teaching and human relations of Jesus, even though no specific saying can be certainly claimed as precisely his, to establish a highly distinctive and unforgettable personality. The large part of the religious and ethical teachings of the first three gospels is surely his in substance, and though it had been rearranged for the uses of the church even before its writing by the evangelists, much of the form of the teaching is little changed. In these stories and impressions there come clear certain features of a religious personality without a counterpart in world history. In this "wine-bibber and glutton," this friend of children and of women, this quick anger and this gift of tears, this earthy man with the raciness and freshness of the poor in his humor, here is a humanity and a warmth which the ascetics and moralists and mystics of religious history cannot match. Buddha, Socrates, Mohammed, Confucius, Plotinus,—none was so lovable or so loved as he. Here also was the gentle strength, the extraordinary sanity and sensitivity required to leave behind a trail of cures among the neurotic and demon-ridden, the psychosomatically disturbed so common in that hysterical atmosphere of Palestine in the decades before the last crazy uprising against Rome.

And yet whoever pitched his demands with such reckless absoluteness? The single-mindedness and renunciation required in the Sermon on the Mount and the parables in the middle of Luke are terrible and ruthless. "Love your enemies and pray for those who persecute you." This in an occupied country seething with revolt! "Give to the man who begs from you." "Whoever strikes you on the right cheek, turn the other to him as well." "Anyone who even looks with lust at a woman has committed adultery with her already in his heart." "Do not trouble about what you are to eat and drink in life, nor about what you are to put on your body." "If anyone comes to me and does not hate his father and mother and wife and children and brother and sister, aye and his own life, he cannot be a disciple of mine . . . so with every one of you who will not part with all his goods—he cannot be a disciple of mine." "You must be perfect, as your father in heaven is perfect." Who else has ever dared to conceive of human life as having these possibilities, save as he has learned of them from these lips? There is no other such absolute program of moral goodness in human history; this is the ultimate, the demand of perfection, and no higher can be conceived. If God wills the active holiness of men, this is the authentic vision.

And yet again, all this comes not in the tone of one laying down unbearable standards, but as a comfort and deliverance, an announcement of a great new release, proclaimed by its messenger in his first reported sermon:

> The spirit of the Lord is upon me:
> for he has consecrated me to preach the
>   gospel to the poor,

he has sent me to proclaim release for captives
   and recovery of sight for the blind,
to set free the oppressed,
   to proclaim the Lord's year of favour.†

Blessing, joy, freedom, peace, the Lord's year of favor!

In this startling and ecstatic assurance of Jesus about the intentions of the deity we find, of course, the explanation for the outrageousness of his demands on human nature. He was well aware that these things are impossible for men. He was also aware that they are possible to God and knew that God was in fact effecting them. This was the very formula of his message, that God was beginning a new creation in man, that the "kingdom" or "reign" was at hand, and in fact already "among you." God was exerting his mercy in a solicitude as of the father of the Prodigal Son; God was breaking the hold of evil on the habits and impulses of men. "Behold, I saw Satan fall as lightning." God was opening to men new dimensions of love and obedience, capacities for goodness they had not before enjoyed. All Jesus' work, his teach-

† Luke 4:18-19, Moffat's translation.

ing, his healing were directed to witness to, to demonstrate, to participate in this new attack of God on the indifference and the estrangement of men. The long-awaited fulfillment of God's promised invasion of mercy, peace, and justice was now begun. When Jesus cast out "demons" it was a manifestation of the healing of the Kingdom. All those superhuman perfections set forth in the Sermon on the Mount—they, too, were manifestations of the new Reign, the new activity of God. When and where any man should be seen completely careless of self in property, reputation, family, seeking only the good of his neighbor, there, surely, was God in act, the present Kingdom. No man out of the Kingdom ever could stand so free of self-assertion.

Precisely how Jesus conceived his own vocation in this fulfillment of the Messianic dream of Judaism is not wholly clear from the Gospels. The resurrection convinced his disciples and the writers of the Gospels that he was precisely the *Messiah*, but evidently the disciples had not believed this during most, if not all, of their association with him. He was for most, if not all, of his career, the

Messiah incognito, known to men as a prophet, a rabbi, a healer. Rembrandt, the great Protestant painter, discerned this mystery of the hidden Christ. Perhaps Jesus himself did not fully realize that he was the Messiah. But he certainly knew that the Messianic age was come, that the Law and the prophets had ceased with John, and that he himself had a unique and terrible responsibility as an agent and bearer of the inbreaking reign of God. Yet the full implication and the precise outcome of his role were possibly not known to him. His work was to obey, and the consequences, ominous as they certainly looked at least toward the end, lay in the hands of the Father. In this case it would be first his disciples who would have the perspective of his completed work in his generation and in the history of redemption. With the key of the resurrection experiences they would discern with certainty that Jesus had been indeed *the* Messiah. And they would legitimately develop his own consciousness that he was an agent of the Kingdom to the assurance that he was the Messianic Suffering Servant who had sealed the new covenant of

God's reign by his death as well as announced it in his preaching.

A degree of human ignorance of the future is certainly apparent in Jesus' foreshortening of the fulfillment of the reign of God. He knew of his personal experience that God had begun his new redemption, and in a sense the measure of the intensity of his sense of God's present power is to be read in his mistaken prophecies of the future. Such was the transforming might he felt about him and in him that he could not but believe that the completion of this warfare was at hand. Some of the prophecies of the imminent end of the world which are put in Jesus' mouth may have been inaccurately read back into him by the disciples and evangelists later, but his whole teaching is steeped in an expectancy and hope which might very naturally have led him to look for the end within the lifetime of that generation, as his disciples report him. Even so this would be a very different view from that of the book of Revelation or of many modern millenarians, who have slipped back into a pre-Christian apocalypticism, losing the sense of the present redeeming power of the Kingdom. Likewise it differs from the other-worldly hope of "Heaven"; the God Jesus served gave himself on this earth in the lives of men and communities, and he was to reign over such. And lastly we might notice that this "Kingdom" was not at all to Jesus an ideal society to be "built" by men, but was the action of God alone in the lives of men, building true brotherhood. No man can build that which by definition is God's building; he can only pray for it and submit himself joyfully to it. Here is the true dynamic of the "social gospel," for which no humanitarian idealism can substitute.

The most striking aspect of the expanding kingdom of God is that of "judgment," of the erection of spiritual and moral norms before which all work-a-day human dealings suddenly stand naked in their meanness, and men are challenged to decision with a new and terrible realization of the urgency and finality and cosmic ramifications of their decision. The negative aspect of judgment, the fires of Gehenna, have seemed rather strong meat to tenderhearted Christians of the last two centuries, but Jesus knew what he was saying.

Why is it that Jews and Christians have never taken any interest in the notion of transmigration of souls, as we find it in Hinduism, Buddhism, or Plato? Surely this is a neater and more manageable speculation than the transfiguration of each and every redeemed person. Yet there is for us, clearly, one crucial inadequacy, its failure to take seriously the ultimacy of the moral decisions within our historical relationships. As heirs of an historical religion, however little we keep of it, we all feel that we are born but once, and decide nearly every day certain issues for ever and with no recurrence.

> Once to every man and nation
> Comes the moment to decide . . .
> And the choice goes by forever
> Twixt that darkness and that light.

In a situation where man must take his place and resolve his destiny in the climactic struggle against God of the powers and principalities of evil, there are consequences possible which shock the tender-minded, but which can be verified in any war or penitentiary. On this matter one is more likely to hear a realism close to that of Jesus from the

Salvation Army than in the sermons attuned to the self-deceptions of our suburban congregations.

His Death and Resurrection

Even more than on the personality and teaching of Jesus, however, has the Christian fellowship dwelt on his passion and death. His last week is the only part of Jesus' lifetime which is traced with some biographical precision by the four Gospels, if not with entire agreement among themselves. Paul, similarly, our earliest witness, apparently assumes the knowledge of Jesus' teaching and healing activities in his readers, but dwells again and again on his passion and resurrection. The Apostles' Creed, likewise, insists only on this in his mortal career, and down through the generations Christians have, of all the Bible, cherished most the passion story, and found their central act of worship in the dramatization of it in the Lord's Supper. What is the full significance of Jesus' suffering and execution in the fulfillment of God's purpose?

Jesus' integrity and refusal to escape death by compromising his vocation raises him, even to the

46

unbeliever, out of the class of uncomprehending sufferers into that of the heroic martyrs. It was no short time during which he wrestled with those perversions of his vocation which, as Dostoievsky's Grand Inquisitor has pointed out, have made their way into the very heart of some of the churches purporting to follow him. He had grown, says the Scripture record, in moral and spiritual stature, from a state of perforce lesser devotion and obedience. "Why callest thou me good," he asked at the height of his ministry, "there is none good save God." It was in heroic dedication to the work of the Kingdom that, after what had happened to John the Baptist, and many another, he set his face to Jerusalem at feast-time, to bear witness to the living God before those who recognized only the power of force or of the kept God of a hierarchy.

How late could Jesus have escaped by denying his trust? We have no means of knowing whether a retirement was still possible in that last week as he sensed the net tightening. Perhaps the night of sweaty prayer in Gethsemane armored him not merely to endure, but also to scorn to make overtures Pilate might have accepted. To the last cry, "My God, why hast thou forsaken me?" the strain was that of a man to whom the day and hour and method of God's vindication were unknown.

The story is of the sketchiest, and we have only the most fragmentary indications of Jesus' thoughts and purposes from the time of his arrival in the city to his death. He had no confidant who perpetuated the inner history of those days, and Christians have always been driven to invest them with feelings and purposes of the personality and teaching they already knew. In itself the passion story cannot compare with the analogous account for Socrates, in Plato's *Apology, Crito,* and *Phaedo,* where the moral grandeur of the protagonist is depicted at length by one of the world's greatest writers. And yet the martyrdom of Jesus has been more fruitful than the more splendidly related martyrdom of Socrates, just in the measure that the new covenant of the living God in history is a mightier power than the most courageous dedication to truth and civic responsibility.

To define the contrast differently, the death of Socrates lies forever on the altar to justice and truth, but the living God *raised* Jesus Christ to serve on with him in his redeeming labor. The risen Christ was seen, says our earliest account, "by Cephas, then by the twelve; after that he was seen by over five hundred brothers all at once, the majority of whom survive to this day, though some have died; after that he was seen by James, then by all the apostles, and finally he was seen by myself." Of the manner of appearance of the risen Christ we have only one firsthand account, that of Paul. What confronted Paul on the Damascus road was no "natural body," of "flesh and blood," and after talking with many other witnesses of the resurrection Paul clearly stated his conviction that the risen Christ could not be of this physical character. Whatever the psychological mechanisms involved, with Paul and with the others (and Paul gives no indications that they were different in the case of the others), God used them to make apparent to these discouraged and bewildered, or even rebellious men, that the new covenant and the new promises taught and manifest in the mortal Jesus were not disrupted but even sealed by his martyrdom, and that Jesus Christ, the bearer

49

of the Kingdom, lived on in power in the continuing work of the Kingdom of redemption. Here is the foundation miracle of Christianity, without which the formation of the Christian fellowship is unintelligible, just as it has been a series of confrontations with the living Christ down the generations which has perpetuated and extended the fellowship of believers. The human prophet and martyr had now "been installed as Son of God with power . . . when he was raised from the dead." Similarly Peter (in his apostolic preaching) fastened on the resurrection as the moment of adoption or transfiguration in which "God has made him both Lord and Christ, this very Jesus whom you have crucified."

CHAPTER FOUR

God's Redemption and Man's Trust

THE SECOND PRINCIPLE OF PROTESTANTISM is
perhaps the most difficult to characterize. It is
inextricable from what has already been said on
the sufficient authority of Christ in history and from
what follows on the church as the dynamic fellowship of reconcilers to that Christ. Yet no
formulation of it has ever commanded such general agreement among all brands of Protestants
as is the case with the evangelical conceptions of
the Word and the Church. It is the evangelical
understanding of the manner of man's redemption, and was usually discussed in the Reformation
century in terms of Paul's and Luther's formula,
"justification by faith," or the Reformed "sovereignty of God." Neither of these phrases satisfied
all Protestants in the sixteenth century, and in

51

some churches of liberal American Protestantism today they are unintelligible. Yet with all the difficulties of vocabulary and the diversities of religious temperament within Protestantism there is here a common ground of conviction and of difficulties which we may be able to suggest if not to define.

The Gift

We may begin with the sovereignty, the kingdom, of God. This resumption of Jesus' favorite term reminds us that the Reformation was first of all no theological or organizational program, but a religious revival. Only because men had the assurance of the presence of God himself, of the return of Christ among them as in Dostoievsky's parable, did they gain the courage to criticize institutions and doctrines long sacrosanct as the appointed ways of man's redemption. God was once again widely apprehended as the actual present ruler of history and nature, and, in particular, in the advance of his Kingdom in the narrower sense of the community of those consciously dedicated to his revealed purpose.

All these ideas were part of the universal doctrine of Christians; what was new was the vividness and the certainty with which they were realized. God was no longer merely the hypothetical "first cause" and sustainer of the elaborate system of natural processes as he had been to the "common sense" view of Aquinas. The physical universe no longer stood in relative independence of God, but became, as it were, transparent and pliable as the glove upon his hand, responsive in every part and event directly to his mysterious will. God was no longer merely the ancient founder of the Church, as if he had set up a trust fund and stated executors with discretionary powers over the distribution of his mercies. No longer was he satisfied to permit such rationing by a legal monopoly. God himself *acted.* He displayed himself not merely as the goal of human idealism and contemplative adoration, but as the Alpha, the living and free initiator and ruler. He had not retired as the Grand Inquisitor supposed, to leave all sovereignty to his viceregents in the hierarchy. He would reign *directly* over the wills of men just as he mastered directly the natural universe. Just as the institutionalism of Judaism had once crumbled before Jesus Christ's disclosure of this God who would not be bottled up either in Jerusalem or in Samaria and would raise up sons of Abraham from the stones, now again his judgment and forgiveness flowed out over sacramental "validities" and proprieties. The Reformation marked the shattering impact of a new actualization of the direct kingship of *God*. The indefinite postponement of this Kingdom which had been the prevailing expectancy since Augustine was now consumed in a new sense of crisis, of urgency, of worlds passing away and being rebuilt as men stood before the ultimate realities. Before this God, man's one security and hope, as in the days of Jesus Christ, lay in the contrite heart and trust in his promises, in "grace alone."

It was this latter human perspective on God's sovereignty in the process of salvation which Luther expressed in a profound reinterpretation of Saint Paul's "justification by faith." Whoever is touched by the widening fellowship of the new covenant knows that his acceptance into it was not earned, that he had not made himself fit to be received by Holiness. Those who have struggled for saintliness, as did Luther and Wesley, know that not only have they fallen short, but that human nature is incapable of saintliness by its own moral resources or by devotion to the sacraments. Men are healed, not by their own struggles for integrity or by mystical raptures, but by the trustful acceptance of what is done for them by God. To be able to trust God is itself a gift of God, and prime evidence of his redeeming activity. The man who can trust discovers that the guilt and viciousness he knows within himself are somehow denatured by a compassion which takes him as he is for what he may be and makes him that.

The great cause of our human resentments and rebellion against the universe, and our reckless fanaticisms, is simply our inability to trust in the reconciliation which is offered to us. We wish it rather on *our* terms, and as *our* achievement. And the relationship of trust is the least subjective, the least man-made of all possible bonds by which we might be linked to the governor of our destiny. Unlike moral self-control or mystical self-manipulation or sacramental prayer wheels, trust recognizes that the power to heal is found only where there is real will to heal, in him who has in fact brought his peace to men and does so still. And here we arrive at the central mystery of the Christian faith, which has never been adequately formulated, of how the heroic life and death of the Lord's perfect servant brings, as it certainly does, the assurance of pardon to sinners, and reconciliation with God. Even the haziest of semi-Christians recognize the power of Jesus' example to shame us in our tepid loyalty and our bland compromises and to inspire us to better living. Jesus brings us closer to God simply by the moral influence of his integrity. But this much we also must in fairness allow to Epictetus and Socrates, and many another hero of the spirit. Christianity has always confessed an obligation of another kind to Jesus Christ. Most of the metaphors used to express it are bizarre or offensive to modern ears in one way or another, "he ransomed us from the devil," he substituted for us in advance in accepting the punishment justice requires for our sins, so that we are washed clean by "the blood of the Lamb." Some of our objections are grounded in good sense, as that to the absurd notion that God and the Devil stand in contractual relations, or that, torn between his justice and his mercy, God indulges in legal chicanery to balance his books. Yet in some way God won a unique victory over the powers of evil through the self-sacrifice of Jesus Christ. At least two elements in these views of Christ's substitution for us, moreover, point to truth, that something objective was accomplished here once for all in God's relations with man and with us, and that, whether we like it or not, vicarious suffering is part of the method of God, here and always.

Some of our objections to vicarious suffering are based on notions of justice, but more of them rest on pride. If anyone insists on suffering for me and then extending me forgiveness, this is adding insult to injury. This is the real reason why again and again I find myself trying to reject the forgiveness and reconciliation offered me in Christ.

Yet the reality and indispensability of vicarious suffering force themselves upon my observations of human relations. How many times have I been restored to balance and flexibility by some friend who stands by, accepting my shame when I am in the wrong, as if to say, "Well, my friend, you have made an outrageous fool of yourself, but I believe in you." Did ever a good parent raise a child without "substituting" for him a hundred times? Is not the prodigal son perennially re-established in dignity by his father's prodigal forgiveness of ingratitude, greed, viciousness? What good is a fine moral example to one who is already embarked obstinately on the road of sin? Sin is not merely the rejection of certain moral standards and a consequent deadening of our insight and aspiration and self-control, but it is also a willful self-isolation. Sin always bars mutuality with some person or persons, as well as with God. The solitary cell in the prison is only the outward symbol of the criminal's inward state, and until that isolation is broken, there is no rehabilitation. To break that isolation is the work of reconciliation by vicarious suffering, to swallow distaste and shame in concern for the prisoned spirit.

That this suffering vicariously is an important element in my own experience I am reluctantly forced to admit. But must I concede this indebtedness to a Jew two thousand years ago who never dreamed of the continent on which I live? Here is the issue of the objectivity of the work and death of Jesus Christ. What was accomplished here? Surely no change in the enduring purpose of God, turning his mind from wrath to forgiveness. Rather the very death of Christ was itself an indispensable part of the disclosure of God's nature and intentions. To the disciples, convinced by the resurrection appearances that Jesus had indeed been the Suffering Servant of God, this was certainty at last that the mercy which he preached and embodied was verily the nature of God himself, whom they could now trust. To me, also, the recognition that in fact God was in Christ reconciling the world, implies that this vicarious suffering to which I acknowledge a debt, is not merely one comforting element in the battleground on which I stand, but is the most powerful factor, being indeed the work of the Kingdom Jesus witnessed to, God still reconciling the world. I am thus bound to Jesus Christ as the announcer, the initiator, the revelation of the work of the living God in pardoning and healing me. And in this way the perfect obedience, the death and resurrection of Christ, were done *for us,* even *in us.* Our mortal lives may continue shabby and unstable so that often we may search ourselves in vain for any signs of the grace to holiness, yet we still cling to the assurance that the objective and eternal and unremitting merciful holiness of God has somehow seized even us and clothed us with the promise of a righteousness beyond our powers of obedience. Our life is no longer merely our empirical all-too-human meanness, but invested in Christ and his Kingdom, in what is done for us and independently of us.

Its Reception

The Reformation insights into God's sovereignty over all created things and his initiative in the redemption of man developed into polemic theological views in two directions. There was first of all an affirmation of God's creative freedom to subdue to himself the free love of man personally with any sort of means. Such a recognition undercut all sacramentalisms and institutionalisms, which always imply limitations of the means God may normally employ. We have had occasion to observe Protestant lapses into institutionalism, bibliolatry, sacramentalism, and other forms of *ersatz* Catholicism; but, in general, Protestantism has been less liable to such tendencies to idolatry and blasphemy, than to the opposite danger of seeing God in no vehicles whatever and fading out into mere secularism. God's freedom to adopt or create any means whatever, ecclesiastical or otherwise, to reconcile man to himself in Christ has remained an enduring Protestant conviction essential to evangelical Christianity.

Divine sovereignty and grace was also emphasized, by Luther and Calvin especially, at the expense of any human contribution to the process of redemption. The Reformation accounts of "justification by faith" remain as classic theological and psychological analyses of the profound spiritual crises of what William James called the "twice-born" men. This type of religious experience gave certitude and power to the great reformers, as it had to Saint Paul before them. But such an experience of God's rescue out of the depth of human frustration and failure cuts across confessional lines. Augustine knew it also and the Dominicans and Augustinians and Jansenists maintained a tradition of salvation by grace alone in the Roman Church, which forced the Council of Trent to straddle the issue while repudiating Lutheran language. Within Protestantism, on the other hand, the humanist and Anabaptist wings did not generally understand the Lutheran and Calvinist depreciation of man's contribution to his own salvation. They recognized the initiative of God in the process, so far as they were evangelicals at all, but they cannot be classified under the Pauline pattern any more than the whole New Testament witness can be reduced to this type. The Quakers felt more affinity to the mystical Johannine view, while many of the Anabaptists and humanists dropped most readily into the moralistic Jewish categories of the first three Gospels. It was not usually a matter of denying the Pauline "justification by faith" so much as a less self-conscious and analytical experience of commitment of the heart and will to God.

With the fading of the vision of the first Reformers, moreover, the general Protestant understanding of salvation went through much the same evolution which occurred in the generations immediately following Paul. The writers of the second century show no comprehension of Paul's intense awareness of the presence and redeeming power of God. Instead of accepting the forgiveness offered in Christ in trust, they set about *earning* their salvation in precisely the Pharisaic style Paul and Jesus had transcended. Tertullian, for example, discusses the penitential acts of a Christian, not as the expression of a contrite heart in gratitude for a forgiveness it could never earn, but as actual compensations and merits before God. Personal religious awareness of God's action faded away and men concentrated more on human responsibility for leading a good life. In the face of Jesus' advice that the best of saints should know themselves "unprofitable servants" and never presume to count their virtues as merits before God like the Pharisee, it was now blandly assumed that men could be good "over and above the commandment of God," and that, on the other hand, the giving of alms to the poor could buy the forgiveness of God for sins. Religion had ceased to be the life of faith in God and became a man-centered cultivation of morality.

Justification by faith was enshrined centrally in the confessions of the chief evangelical churches, but there is no institutional way of preserving the religious insight itself. "Faith" came increasingly to revert to its "Catholic" meaning of "assent to propositions" in place of trust in a personal God, and "justification by faith" was then a justification which could be earned by human effort—precisely what Paul and Luther had intended to preclude by the phrase in the first place. Luther had returned again and again to the fundamental contrast between the two types of faith:

There are two kinds of believing: first a believing about God which means that I believe that what is said of God is true. This faith is rather a form of knowledge than a faith. . . . Men possessing it can say, repeating what others have said: I believe that there is a God. I believe that Christ was born, died, rose again for me. But what the real faith is, and how powerful a thing it is, of this they know nothing . . . they think that faith is a thing which they may have or not have at will, like any other natural human thing; so when they arrive at a conclusion

64

and say, "Truly the doctrine is correct, and therefore, I believe it," then they think that this is faith.

When faith is of the kind that *God* awakens and creates in the heart, then a man trusts in Christ. He is then so securely founded on Christ that he can hurl defiance at sin, death, hell, the devil, and all God's enemies. He fears no ill, however hard and cruel it may prove to be . . . such faith which throws itself upon God, whether in life or in death, alone makes a Christian man. . . . It kills the past and reconstitutes us utterly different men in heart, disposition, spirit, and in all the faculties. . . . Oh! there is something vital, busy, active, powerful about this faith that simply makes it impossible ever to let up in doing good works. The believer does not stop to ask whether good works are to be done, but is up and at it before the question is put. . . . Faith is a lively, reckless confidence in the grace of God . . . so it is that a man unforced acquires the will and feels the impulse to do good to everybody, serve everybody and suffer everything for the love and praise of God who has bestowed such grace upon him. . . . Pray to God that he work this faith in you: otherwise you will never, never come by it, feign all that you will or work all you can.*

* Lindsay, T. M., *History of the Reformation,* Vol. I (New York: Chas. Scribner's Sons, 1912), pp. 429, 430, 431, 445.

Despite such warnings, Lutherans and Calvinists worked all they could and feigned all they would as if faith were a thing they might have or have not at will, and were able to deny the very meaning of justification by faith while insisting with fanaticism on its words. Thus was the ground laid for the triumph of rationalism and moralism in the eighteenth century. Modern Protestantism has known nearly as many attempts as modern Romanism to supplement or replace the Reformation justification by faith with descriptions taking their departure from human freedom and responsibility. Religious revivals within Protestantism, to be sure, seem usually to return to the Pauline view, but it would not be accurate to call this the universally accepted Protestant interpretation of the way of salvation in either the twentieth or the sixteenth century. In both centuries, however, this has probably been the dominant Protestant interpretation. "Catholicism," on the other hand, has never been able to repudiate it fully. In the first decades of the Reformation, negotiators who hoped to heal over the split found this one of the areas most amenable to adjustment. And in our own day, at the Edinburgh Conference in 1937, Protestants, Orthodox, and Anglo-Catholics were happy to discover that they could phrase a mutually satisfactory statement on God's grace and man's free response in the process of salvation. Perhaps it would be fair to state that with regard to the manner of man's reconciliation, Protestants agree that God is the initiator and aggressive agent, with a sovereign and unlimited choice of means at his disposal, but are not entirely agreed as to precisely how much or what kind of freedom man exercises in his response to God.

CHAPTER FIVE

The Protestant Conception of the Church

FROM THE GOOD NEWS of new health for humanity we may turn to the community which actualizes this message, and a third Protestant conception, the frequently misunderstood "priesthood of all believers." This conception constitutes still an unsurmountable hurdle for all efforts toward unity with Orthodox or with Roman Catholics.

Evangelical Fellowship

Protestants as well as their opponents have often represented this principle to mean simply the religious emancipation of the individual, as if to say, "every man his own priest." That emphasis on the inescapable responsibility of every individual to come to terms with God personally is indeed intended here, but this is not the primary weight of the principle. The wider meaning is rather "every man his neighbor's priest," or, to drop the term "priest," "the mutual ministry of all believers." The formula is thus in reality equivalent to Luther's favorite description of the church, "the communion of saints," meaning by "saints" not men who had achieved moral perfection, but those who were saved by trust, "believers." "Mutual ministry," however, expresses more emphatically than "communion," the dynamic character of the Christian fellowship.

Paul, the great missionary to the non-Jewish world, first discussed the nature of this new creation, the church. The church was to continue the labor of Jesus, preaching the Kingdom and actually bringing it by mediating God's forgiveness and reconciliation. She was defined, consequently, as a second incarnation, a body whose indwelling spirit is that of the resurrected Christ. There are two characteristics of this continuing apostolate of the Kingdom, the extraordinary mutuality and fellowship which comes from the constant ministry one to another of God's forgiveness, and the con-

69

tinual sense of dependence on the spirit of Christ. "As the human body is one and has many members, all the members of the body forming one body for all their number, so is it with Christ. For by one Spirit we have all been baptized into one Body, Jews or Greeks, slaves or freemen . . . thus, if one member suffers, all the members share its suffering; if one member is honored, all the members share its honor." Through all the scattered brotherhoods in the cities of Asia Minor, Europe, and Africa there was this vivid sense of being *one* chosen community, overriding all distinctions of neighborhood, class lines, nationality, or culture. A man did not think of himself primarily as a member of this or that particular local church, as do so many American Protestants, but as a member of Christ's one body.

The blessings of Christian fellowship are not once received and then passively enjoyed. The primary function of that fellowship is to transmit God's reconciling love in the lives and words of its members, and so long as the fellowship remains in Christ, that process is continuous. We may bring in here still a third emphasis much

70

used by the Reformers. There is a true portion of the church of Christ, they said, wherever the message of redemption in Christ is truly presented in preaching, in the sacraments, or in men's lives and *where it is received.* The ministering thus must be effective, must kindle like fire and evoke kindred response before we are sure God is in the work. The highly corporate emphasis of all these terms shows the Reformation protest against the individualism of late medieval Catholicism. Evangelical Protestantism means "social religion"; as John Wesley was to say later, it means communion, mutual ministry, the sharing of the most sacred things in life, it means the Body of Christ, the Church. Calvin thus takes up the saying of the early church, "No man can have God for his father who has not the Church for his mother." And Luther likewise directed, "Anyone who is to find Christ, must first find the Church." He is not to "trust to himself, nor by the help of his own reason build a bridge of his own to heaven" but to unite with the people who believe in Christ. Outside the actual fellowship of those who live to Christ, the living Christ is not to be discovered.

And within this fellowship of believers the first Protestant virtue is mutuality, in contrast to the primary Romanist virtue, submission.

The fellowship of Christians can be defined as the community of the forgiven and forgiving. They are a company exclusively of sinners, but their rebellion and estrangement from God and each other and from their own consciences has been overcome. Only as overcome, in fact, are Christians able to face themselves in their full stature as sinners, for without a presentiment of a pardon our instinct of moral self-preservation would not permit this confession. No one ever explores so much of hell as the saints, for they alone dare to lay bare in themselves levels of self-assertion and malignancy whose very existence the merely respectable man would deny. The redeemed can afford to admit guilt and thereby to burst the psychic bonds of evil. They can even assume the shame of others, binding themselves to the guilt of men about them with whom they live in natural associations. God sets this community of thieves to catch more thieves.

In every nation and continent there are cells of

this hidden fifth column, this leaven in which the community building powers of the Kingdom are at work, and where also is hardened the courage to say "No!" when necessary, to the demands of nation, race, or class. Taking up into their own hearts the terrible tensions of our age, accepting the weight of oppression and exploitation, or perhaps the retribution long due their nation or race or class, and by their bruises, healing—such are the faithful. We do not know who they are, save as we hear of a handful here and a couple there, but we know they are there and everywhere as the chosen of God unto whom the spirit of Christ Jesus is close. In our day, especially, their labors of pity and mercy are often but half-consciously "in the name of Christ." They are the quickest discovered under persecution, when their quiet endurance singles them out from the bitter and violent and weak. In the success of good causes, on the other hand, they are usually unidentified among the fair-weather virtuous and those who make a living jumping on bandwagons. Unto them alone is committed the "power of the keys" of heaven and hell, for by their testimony to justice and mercy they condemn the wicked, and by their forgiveness they heal the repentant and bring them to eternal life. In the irrevocable decisions for or against the Kingdom are men thus bound or loosed to eternity.

We have been speaking not of the churches, but of the Church, those in whom the spirit of the Messiah, the Suffering Servant, dwells and labors at his reconciliation today. This is the true Christian fellowship, created by a call and nourished by the living word, in which all are members one of another and the head is Christ. To apply this description to any church congregation or institution in America or elsewhere would provoke a smile, and indeed it should. The churches manifest extremely little of Christ's passionate reconciling aggressiveness. As institutions many of them seem to be rather associations of idealists, dedicated to the "ethics of Jesus," or organizations for the perpetuation of this or that creedal statement or liturgical practice or form of government. No such institution should be taken for the Church, yet most of them in their pathetic ways bear witness to the Kingdom down the generations, the memory of its beginning, the disturbing sense of its hidden presence, the hope of its perfection into which the churches may dissolve. And for this interim the churches with all their tepidity and unfaithfulness are necessary. They represent the culture, so to speak, of the Holy Spirit, and preserve an infinitely precious tradition. One needs to steep himself in that culture, its Bible, its hymns, its liturgy and prayer, its music and art, its creeds and theology, to learn the full richness of God's revelation. And yet to serve the true Church and its Lord, we must also be merciless on the churches, that is, on ourselves.

Ministry, Word, and Sacraments

Let us then review the several agencies and aspects of the institutional churches from this Protestant understanding of the true Church. The ministry, the preaching of the Word, the sacraments, the government of the church may all be touched on here. The Bible as a means of grace will be treated in the next chapter.

The principle of the mutual ministry of believers has implications, first of all, for the status

75

and functions of the Protestant clergy. The Protestant clergyman can never claim the distinct spiritual status and the peculiar prerogatives of a priest in the Orthodox or Roman Catholic sense. On all fundamental matters he is only another "believer," of the same rank with the "ministers" in the pews. Not all men and women in the Christian fellowship have the qualities of mind and body to conduct public worship effectively, to preach, to interpret the Scriptures profitably at some length, to conduct sacraments with dignity and beauty. Some of these functions also require special training. The evangelical clergyman, however, performs them all only in a representative capacity for the fellowship; he is articulating the life animating all. The ministrations of the clergyman, in fact, may not be the most effective expression of the reconciling power in the community. By the visible integrity of their lives, housewives may often minister Christ more effectively to each other than can a clergyman whose housekeeping experience is desultory. As Luther has it, all believing laymen "are worthy to appear before God, to pray for others, to teach each other mutually the things that are of God . . . so ought we freely to help our neighbors by our body and our works, and each should become to the other a sort of Christ, so that we may be mutually Christs, and that the same Christ may be in all of us." The Quakers make the point clear by exaggerating it. They have no permanent ministry (in their classical type); the message of the Word is spoken in their meetings by whoever feels a vocation to the public ministry on that particular occasion.

At the other extreme from the Friends, the Anglicans, Presbyterians and Reformed, and some Lutherans maintain an exalted conception of the role of the regular evangelical ministry. Though all believers are truly and equally ministers of Christ, the regular clergy perform highly significant functions. They are, for example, by far the strongest force for continuity in the Christian fellowship down the generations. They are equipped by special training to reinterpret the experience and tradition of the fathers both as guide and corrective to the passing moods and enthusiasms of the rising generations, in theology or worship or ethics. Through the trained clergy the local congregations have what is normally their sole avenue to the aspirations and failures, the holiness and struggles of generations of Christians who lived by faith and were not to be perfected apart from us. To the local congregation, again, it is the regular minister who in overwhelming degree represents the larger church of the present generation. He has been ordained, as a rule, at the hands of other clergy. Through him come the relations with administrative bodies for the common enterprises of local congregations, missions, religious education, philanthropies, and the like. Whether he intends it or not, the minister represents in his person the whole Church, living and dead, to his congregation, and in particular the actively evangelistic apostolate of the believing community, reaching back in unbroken continuity to the disciples. His own character and spiritual gifts and insights are highly important, yet he never speaks from them alone.

By thus representing the whole Church, finally, the regular clergy constitute the focus of Christian independence of cultural movements, nationalistic, political, social. Just as the regular clergy of the primitive church crystallized partly out of the need of the Christian movement to consolidate against cultural perversions and political persecution of the faith, so the analogous pressures in our day are leading Protestants to recast their thinking on the nature of the ministry. The historic episcopate of the Anglicans or the succession of ordaining presbyters among the Reformed, together with their administrative functions, need to be measured anew by the jealously laic wing of Baptists, Disciples, and Congregationalists who have perhaps oversimplified the priesthood of all believers.

The "mutual ministry of all believers," of course, undercuts also the priestly monopoly of the means of God's mercy. The Anglo-Catholic, Orthodox, and Roman sacraments are "valid" only when performed under certain rigid conditions and by certain qualified priests. Were these churches to admit the priesthood of all, they must then concede that the sacraments only mediate, if in heightened vividness and concentration, the same reconciliation of God mutually ministered within the fellowship, and that thus they are not absolutely indispensable. This they cannot admit. The apostolic and evangelical sacraments are vehicles of the free personal love of God, but the Catholic views the grace received as an impersonal *thing*, like a blood transfusion whose virtue is independent of the personal relations of donor and recipient.

In the Protestant conception, the ecclesiastical sacraments are solemn, dramatic, and corporate manifestations of the *same mercies*. What is offered in the preaching of the Word is Christ. What is offered in the Lord's Supper is Christ. In the joy of the vindication of the resurrection they remember the obedience unto death which sealed the new covenant and rejoice in the experience of Christ's continued fellowship. To this very day in the evangelical Lord's Supper the experience of the disciples at Emmaus is repeated again and again. Men have departed from the table-fellowship of Christians with a sudden recognition that the living Christ has been present among them, and have said to each other in wondering joy, "Did not our hearts glow within us?" The consecration of the brotherhood to the mind of Christ, as his new body, is symbolized here, and also the mutuality within the group. This participation of the community in the sacraments meant the great sacramental revival of the Reformation in which Luther and Calvin urged the weekly observance of the Lord's Supper by all after the manner of the early church. Prayers and Scripture also were in a language everyone could understand, and there could be genuine participation by the laity.

And perhaps most important of all was the recovery of the congregational singing of the ancient church. The prescribed Gregorian chant, denied to the laity, was now replaced by free congregational participation. The austere beauty of the Genevan psalms with Bourgeois' music, and the rich flowering of Lutheran hymnody mark the recovery of a corporate spirit and a new richness in worship, despite the elimination of saints and censers.

Church Government

As to the organization and government of the institutional church, the priesthood of all means

81

the participation of all believers in government. With modern Rome "the church," practically speaking, means the clergy (if not the pope, on the principle, *l'église c'est moi*). The laity are purely passive in administration as in teaching. But where all believers are "priests," the government of the church cannot be absolutist, but must be representative from the local congregation to the whole church catholic.

The very notion of an enduring community down the ages had, of course, no place in the thought of Jesus. He sent messengers to preach the news that the Reign of God was at hand, and apparently felt that there was scarcely time to reach the tribes of Israel. There was neither time nor purpose for a settled institution, and as for government among his followers, James and John were rebuked for asking for some of the prerogatives later claimed by the bishops of Rome. Jesus gathered the men who were to minister in the church, but its birthday came after his resurrection, at Pentecost. It was the risen Christ, not the mortal Jesus, who laid on the disciples the injunction to preach to all nations, and this leading of his Spirit was only gradually accepted by them, as Paul's struggles demonstrate.

The early churches lived like those on the American frontier. There were no trained and established clergy; little companies were gathered here and there by circuit-riding evangelists, Paul, Prisca, Aquila, Apollos. What organization they had was usually on the synagogue pattern where an executive committee or sanhedrin of elders, also called "bishops" and "presbyters," carried on the necessary administrative responsibility. It was the traveling evangelists and prophets who were the spiritual authorities. Some of them, however, evidently abused the confidence placed in them, and the churches began to feel an increasing need for a criterion for testing spiritual claims. The local elders gained weight as stabilizing influences in proportion as the claims of missionary evangelists came under closer scrutiny. The pattern of local government, however, was not everywhere the same. Some churches, like Corinth and Rome, evidently were directed by a board of elders into the second century, while at Antioch responsibility was concentrated early in the single pastor.

The superior efficiency of the latter procedure was doubtless the chief factor in its widespread adoption in the second century. There are thus historical precedents in the early church for the Congregational and Baptist type of church organization as well as the Presbyterian. And while diocesan bishops of the modern Episcopal and Roman Catholic type were not developed for many generations, nevertheless the high-church claim for the divine authority of the clergy over the laity finds a very early expression in Ignatius of Antioch. Historical scholarship recognizes a limited validity to all these claims and by that fact denies the possibility of any one validly to assert exclusive divine sanction for itself. The debates over the proper organization of the churches must be settled on other grounds.

An institutional and external conception of the succession from the apostles also developed in the early period. There was grave need, as we have seen, for some criterion of evangelical faith and practice amid the controversies, and those churches, like Jerusalem, Antioch, Rome, and Alexandria, whose local traditions went back to the earliest days, were looked to for guidance. The opinions of those apostolic foundations carried such weight that it became very important to demonstrate the antiquity and continuity of their traditions. Much as newly rich families suddenly acquire descent from Richard the Lionhearted or William the Conqueror, so lists of the succession of bishops in Rome and elsewhere now appeared as credentials. Out of recollections of names of earlier elders, for example, the Roman church pieced together an unbroken line back to "bishop" Peter. The episcopal status, and even the existence of these "bishops," of course, was highly dubious for the period anterior to the memories of the living generation.

The pastor of the Roman congregation, however, had other recommendations than the inherited mantles of both Peter and Paul. He presided over the largest and wealthiest congregation of the Christian world, and one made up, as was natural in the capital city, of members transferred from other congregations all over the empire. He was consequently called upon to arbitrate differences between congregations more often than

85

the others. Men who supported this leadership of the bishop of Rome, like Irenaeus and Cyprian, however, never hesitated to call him to account when he, too, fell into error on interpretations of the faith, and Alexandria, Antioch, and Jerusalem, especially, defended jealously their equal claims to apostolic authority.

Some ingenious lawyer apparently invented the argument for Roman supremacy in the third or fourth century. It all rested on a new interpretation of that passage in Matthew (16: 18, 19) which follows Peter's first profession of conviction that Jesus was the Messiah. The words of Jesus in reply are, "Now I tell you, Peter is your name, and on this rock (Greek "petra") I will build my church. . . . Whatever you prohibit on earth will be prohibited in heaven, and whatever you permit on earth will be permitted in heaven." The majority of fathers, ancient and medieval, agreed that the cornerstone referred to in this passage meant the conviction that Jesus was the Messiah, and that to the whole fellowship sharing that conviction was given the authority of the "power of the keys." The new interpretation, however, urged that it was Peter himself who was made cornerstone and authority for the church, and that when he died this authority was somehow transmitted to the bishops of Rome in succession.

In reaction against this whole tendency to solidify the church into a "battalion of bishops," as Tertullian expressed it, there arose major revolts. While these schismatic groups, like many such, went to fanatical extremes, they also embodied a genuine evangelical appeal to the priesthood of all believers and a warning to all regularly ordained clergy that the true apostolic succession lies not in external and official devolution from the apostles, but in being like them.

When the monarchical papacy recaptured the machinery of church government in the late middle ages, the conciliar tradition of representative democracy was forced into Protestantism. This is the significance of the Reformation in constitutional history. All the Reformers appealed to a free general assembly of the church to arbitrate on the issues of the Reformation, but the papacy knew better than to permit such an assembly. When the Council of Trent was finally summoned, it had been carefully rigged and was expertly steered. Rome has feared nothing more than a free general council since the middle of the fifteenth century, even if its attendance is to be limited to Romanists.

On Protestant soil, however, the representative principle was consistently applied to local units and up to the largest units feasible. Only the Calvinist churches were able to carry through this pattern on a national and occasionally international scale. The separatists desired no government beyond that of the independent congregations, and the Lutherans and Anglicans were inhibited by political interference. Luther's original intentions for the German evangelicals were apparently equivalent to the pattern later worked out by the Calvinists, but the disorder of the class wars of the first decade of the Reformation convinced him that responsible and stable Christians were too rare in the congregations to risk it. Thus the use of evangelical princes as "emergency bishops" in the Lutheran churches became permanent and both congregational and synodical life was precluded until Lutheranism in America should one day have freedom to develop on principles congenial to the mutual ministry of all believers. The Anglicans, likewise, found their church organization captured by the monarchy, and both national and diocesan assemblies were prohibited altogether for generations. Even in our own day the control of Anglican affairs by a parliament including dissenters, atheists, and Jews, and the appointment of governing bishops by non-Anglican prime ministers have raised grave questions.

The Protestant principle of representative government is not to be understood as a replacing of the divine right of the pope by a divine right of the people, or of the majority. Representative government can make mistakes; it is not infallible. But just because it recognizes its fallibility, it provides means for retrieving its errors. All Protestant assemblies of dignitaries may err, and sometimes do. Recognizing this possibility, they do not make the irrecoverable and appalling errors of the "infallible" papacy, nor with the Orthodox, bind all generations absolutely to the theological vocabulary of the fourth and fifth centuries.

CHAPTER SIX

The Bible

TO MANY IT IS ODD or even offensive that the crucial knowledge of God should be found in a book, printed by this or that firm, sold over the counter, read to tatters or left on a parlor table to petrify. God should use more dignified means, and much less particular ones, at least sermons in stones and running brooks if not the pillars of cloud and fire. He should have inscribed his purposes in the consciences of all men, or at least all the philosophers, or made them apparent in the unchanging majesties of nature. A book is so much subject to circumstance, so outrageously unique and specific a channel for universal truth!

The fact that the true understanding of God should be found in a mere book, however, is a necessary consequence if God has revealed himself in history, since a history must be recorded. And this is the chief ground of offense. Most of the world's higher religions and nearly all of the world's classical philosophies proceed on the contrary assumption, that the nature of ultimate reality and of man's adjustment to it are unaffected by the transitory and unsystematic ebb and flow of history. Man finds God perhaps by ceasing to concern himself with historical activity, by rising in contemplative abstraction to the unchanging absolutes, accounting the world of events *Maya* or illusion. Or, if more actively inclined, he finds principles of decision in eternal and universal moral laws of conscience as with Kant and the Stoics. There is something arbitrary in the contention of the historical religions that God himself is concerned with that conflict of wills and community purposes which make history, and that certain human purposes are more directly related to *his* purposes than those of other communities. As the old line runs:

> How odd
> that God
> should choose
> the Jews.

Human history, however, is generally arbitrary and "undemocratic" in these matters. Nine-tenths of those who assert that all the higher religions teach the same truths are only voicing their prejudice against the actual variety and inequality of human history, and have not, in fact, studied the character of any of the higher religions. Anyone who has ever been touched by prophetic religion and wishes to learn the ways of God with human communities, will read the history of the Hindus and Greeks and Egyptians and Chinese with dissatisfaction and meager profit, and even despite himself return to the Jews and that greatest of Jews in the world's unique sourcebook of the redemption of history, the Bible.

The passing away of the personal friends of Jesus made the recording of memoirs about him essential, and various collections of deeds and sayings were compiled in diverse places. The earliest of our present gospels, that of Mark, was composed at the end of this first generation, very possibly incorporating earlier documents. Luke, still later, described how he had gathered the accounts of several writers together, and that Matthew did the same is evident from his incorporation of nearly all the text of Mark. Other gospels were also compiled, some of which we know in scraps and fragments, and various churches in various parts of the Mediterranean world treasured one or another of these accounts. The latest gospel was that of John, written about the beginning of the second century.

Many discordant groups were making the claim, repeatedly used down the centuries and not least by Rome, that their peculiar conceptions were founded on unwritten teachings of Jesus, whether preserved by oral tradition or communicated in visions. The variegated literature as to the nature of Jesus' gospel required sifting so that an agreement could be secured as to which books and interpretations were to be approved for public worship. The first fruits of this process of "higher criticism" was a consensus on four of the many gospels in circulation as being the most reliable, together with the letters of the apostle Paul. The nucleus of a "new testament" to set beside the Jewish testament was established. All private revelations and traditions must henceforth be measured by this common and objective standard, the historical record of God's revelation in Jesus Christ. The second century church was thus forced to the Protestant insight that the only criterion of conflicting traditions or illuminations by the Inner Light is history, the Bible, the earliest and best records of God's work in Christ. This does not mean that the Bible is necessarily the primary means by which men are first brought to the gospel. On the contrary, the Reformers emphasized that men first find the gospel in the living tradition of the church, in the lives of believing parents or friends. And only so are men brought to understand the Bible, through the living fellowship and in it. And yet time and again that living tradition must be judged and reformed by the final authority in Christianity, the gospel.

It is often said that the Reformation simply substituted an infallible Bible for an infallible Pope, a formula which is incorrect on both counts. The popes were not generally regarded as infallible before the Reformation, and the Reformation did not acknowledge an infallible Bible. The Reformers simply asserted the traditional Christian conception that the Word of God in the Bible must be the last court of resort in the church. They applied this criterion more radically, to be sure, to widespread abuses than had been done before. The fundamental novelty with regard to the problem of authority which the sixteenth century produced was the new and unprecedented decision rendered by the Council of Trent. This was the council which gathered to reorganize the Roman church in defense against the Reformation just four hundred years ago. So radical was its reorganization that one may well ask the modern Romanist, "Where was your church before Trent?" To the dismay of its more sober members, the Council of Trent, for the first time in Christian history, set up "tradition" as of "equal" authority to the Bible. Well might Bishop Ken speak of "the new Trent religion."

The content of this tradition acclaimed as of equal authority with the revelation of God in Christ is variegated. Many elements of popular paganism had pressed their way into the post-Constantinian church and were domesticated as the "veneration" of saints, relics, and particularly the Virgin Mary. Many of the "saints" were local pagan deities and still today, in such places as Latin America, one finds extraordinary fusions of heathenism with a Catholic veneer. The case of the Virgin Mary, however, is most serious, since she has in actual practice replaced Jesus Christ as the mediator between man and God for millions of Roman Catholics everywhere.

The sanction of Rome supports the affirmations of theologians who deny that any man can be saved without the protection of the Virgin, and assert that even God obeys her "command." What a fall is here from the preaching of repentance and the perfect holiness of the Kingdom! The reconciliation brought by Jesus Christ is indissoluble from his known historical character and absolute spiritual and ethical demands. Mary announced no Kingdom of the living God and her historical character neither is nor can be known. Jesus the Christ alone has power to forgive sin, but the cult of Mary is based on the superstition that she can obtain for men release from the *consequences* of sin. This is the fundamental perversion of the gospel which has tainted the adoration of the Virgin and the saints from its inception and against which Protestantism must ever maintain the purity and unequaled authority of God's revelation in Christ. The bishops of Trent exalted this kind of tradition as a new and equal revelation with the gospel. Among Roman Catholics, fortunately, there are thousands who are content to say simply, "I am of Christ."

The history of Tridentine Romanism (that is, the Romanism of Trent) has elucidated the consequences of that fatal error of Trent. Once committed to extra-Biblical tradition as actual revelation, the manifold disagreements within the tradition have pushed Romanists inescapably to the last step, the definition that the final authority and revelation of the church is neither Biblical nor traditional but the mere say-so of the current pope-king. Thus when Pius IX was reproached with the historical fact that tradition witnessed without disagreement for over a thousand years against the infallibility of the pope, for the definition of which he was scheming, he replied, "I am tradition."

And yet the Bible is a difficult book for the modern educated man to read. Our very training in critical scientific thinking has strangely handicapped us in our attempts to interpret the idiom of imaginative writing of the pre-scientific age. The habit of scientific thought, precise, colorless, literal, gives us great powers of manipulating our environment, but it inhibits our understanding and our own deepest self-expression. We cannot handle symbolism and imagery confidently. We would like to believe that everything of meaning in religious symbols can be stated boldly in propositions to which one may say "Yes" or "No." At least this is what has been very widely done to the Bible in the last three hundred years, both by those who have said "Yes" and by those who have said "No." Thus great numbers have taken it as literally and crassly meant that God walked in the garden and the serpent spoke with an audible voice, and that Joshua stalled the whirling cosmos and Jonah, like Pinocchio, survived the digestive fluids of the whale, and have supposed, furthermore, that one must believe all this and more or be no Christian. The literal and precise temper of modern science has thus conquered the very people who supposed they were defending the faith against science. They were betrayed by an overly rationalistic and utilitarian education into a fundamental misunderstanding of what they held most sacred, defending what was untenable and worthless and often losing what was most true and important.

A wooden and literal interpretation of the Bible, however, is often no worse than an allegorical exegesis which seeks the same goal of reducing the whole literature to theological and scientific propositions. According to the procedure advocated by Thomas Aquinas, for example, every passage of Scripture bears three types of allegorical sense besides its straightforward literal meaning. By means of these several types of allegory, a variety of doctrinal and moral theses can be extracted from any passage by the exercise of moderate ingenuity. When the literal meaning seems to conflict with what the present pope enjoins, then the interpreter must understand an orthodox allegorical sense to be the true meaning of the passage. By this type of interpretation the fundamental historical character of the Bible can be lost altogether in the intoxicating exercise of uncontrolled allegorizing. If a mischievous demon were to convert the pope to Islam or Buddhism, some loyal Jesuit would surely extract either system from the Scriptures in good faith on Thomist principles. Books can be written, to be sure, with all four levels of meaning, as Dante proved in his *Divine Comedy.* But with the exception of a few books like the Gospel of John, or Revelation, the Bible was *not* written on four levels, or in allegorical style. The simple historical meaning is the intended meaning in the great majority of cases, and the Reformation reading of it so in the believing community brought to light the unity and coherence of the Bible as the makers of the canon saw it.

The fundamental error in this method of Biblical interpretation is the attempt to deduce from the Bible a comprehensive and closed system of philosophical and dogmatic truths, instead of letting the Bible speak in its own terms. Any such static syllabus will possess elements which will conflict with other knowledge in the progress of science and will become simply incredible. In the literalist or Romanist conception they must nevertheless be affirmed by Christians by some "sacrifice of the intellect." But Christianity is not a philosophy, although it has prompted many philosophies. Much less is it an astronomy or geology. It does not matter to Christianity whether the earth was created in six days or six billion, whether it rests on pillars with water above the sky, or whether this fellow Copernicus is right after all. A believing Christian can well afford to be agnostic over very extensive ranges of subjects, including even such as the reasons for suffering and sin, for the inequalities of human destiny, spiritual as well as physical, the nature of life after death, hell-fire, the fate and meaning of the unredeemed and of the vicious, angels, demons, many types of alleged miracles. Our own experience of growing insight should warn us against hasty dogmatic rejections, and we should always hold our minds open on elements which are, or have been, significant to others in the Christian fellowship. The great central affirmations, how-

ever, are those by which men live, and if we have
adequate direction for our living in this confusing
world, we do not need to have it all explained.
Christianity does not pretend to explain it; Christianity is not a "system," it is a commitment, a
community of faith.

The History of Redemption

If we are able to free ourselves of this habit of
treating the Bible as a manual of science, philosophy and ethics we will be on the way to an
understanding of the principle on which it was
assembled, and for which it should be read. Unlike Greek or Hindu myths, which illustrate
eternal truths, the Biblical accounts trace specific
and unique dealings with men of the living God.
And as befits the living God, the dominant literary
structure of the Bible and of the Christian self-
consciousness in general is not philosophical medi-
tation or ethical discourse, but narration, the
account of what God has *done* at certain times and
places. Even genealogies and priestly enthusiasms
about liturgical equipment have their place in the
Bible in so far as they contribute to an under-

standing of the meeting of God's will and man's, of that series of rebellions, reconciliations, promises, punishments which the Bible contains. God acts in all history, of course, but it is in this particular history that his presence and purpose in the face of human indifference, defiance and obedience are uniquely exposed because of the unique awareness of this people, or some among them. All men see the unending rise and decline of the peoples of this world, and many hold it meaningless. It is as if the writers of Scripture viewed the crumbling cities through glasses polarized to reveal the devouring flame of divine judgment invisible to the naked eye. With such an insight of the living God at work, the relation of this particular people to him was lifted to a new dimension of consciousness both in its reverence and in its apostasy. Those who have glimpsed Jehovah trampling the winepress, or gathering his sheep as a shepherd can never make their day-to-day decisions in the innocence of earlier days.

We can recover some sense of how the Bible was written and how it was read in a pre-scientific Christianity by listening to preaching like that of

Green Pastures. Much preaching in quasi-illiterate communities is a dramatic expansion on the Bible stories, into which the congregation enters even audibly, done with considerable freedom and no literalistic inhibitions. The book itself is no infallible and untouchable record. Rather the Bible drops away as a prompting script, and its characters are felt as real and living persons—Joshua, Moses, Jesus, Paul. Their histories are told over with all sorts of variations and even humor within the believing congregation. God himself is realized as a present "person" even while the weight of his judgment is brought home, and the wonder of his forgiveness. The whole interpretation is in many ways similar to some of the more reverent medieval mystery plays. The congregation has a tact for the religious essence of the story, and is quite careless about literal exactitude in details. Though no doubt is felt about the historical truth of the account, critical standards of precise and verified history are not understood or applied.

This is the type of group tradition of which most of our Bible is the written record, and for the re-enactment of which the Bible has served down through many centuries in the Christian fellowship. We moderns are baffled by it because we have almost entirely lost the practice of congregational revivification whereby the Bible becomes again a prompter's script for the dialogue of man and God. We can neither dismiss the Bible as wholly legendary nor, on the other hand, rest confident in it as scientifically true when we regard it primarily as a body of information and propositions. Truly we must become again as little children (through whatever process of sophistication) before we can enter the Kingdom of religious and artistic communication and understanding.

Our evangelical understanding of the nature of the Church, however, prepares us for the reception of the disclosure of God through the Scriptures. We are from the beginning free from the dead hand of a tradition or an authority claiming finality. All branches of Christendom have always held the Bible to be in some sense authoritative, and all branches ancient and modern, except Romanism, have always urged lay reading of the Bible. Different answers, and different kinds of answers, however, have been given to the question, "Who is to interpret the Scriptures?" "Only the hierarchy with the pope," says Rome, "and in the light of the fathers so far as they can be represented as being in accord with the reigning pope." And while Eastern Orthodoxy encourages far greater latitude in popular devotions, on major controversies her churches too would reply, "Only by the hierarchy so far as it agrees with the consensus of the fathers."

What of Protestantism? Here the "mutual ministry of believers" implies an answer of a different type. There is no institutionally located static authority. Like the church itself, authoritative interpretation is a dynamic process. The Scriptures are interpreted out of the shared experience of the believing community, the Holy Spirit witnessing in each and in each to each other of the truth of what is intended *for us*. By means of the scholarship of the learned men in the fellowship, the views of the fathers are also contributed to the conversation, on the principle, as T. S. Eliot puts it, of "giving the dead a vote," but not as infallible opinions. Every individual believer is both expositor and learner of the message of salvation, and while some are always granted more weight at any given time than others, none are infallible and none are to be dismissed without a hearing.

The Reformation marked a tremendous flowering of group study of the Bible. Nearly every Protestant hearth became the seat of a permanent seminar on the significance of the daily family readings, and the varieties of prayer meetings and reading circles have been endless. The only secure position with regard to the Word is joyful humble participation in the common effort of the Christian fellowship to search and to obey. Time and again this Protestant method of seeking the will of God for his people has led to disagreement. So long as the disagreement is contributed in humility to the mutual ministrations of the Word within the enduring fellowship, that is as it should be. As soon as any one formulation is removed from discussion and set up as final, then evangelical Protestantism has been abandoned for a substitute institutionalism.

No person public nor private, nor any church

can claim of itself the prerogative of final determination of God's Word. All Protestant creedal formulations and theologies, so long as they are Protestant, must be tentative in this sense, always standing under correction of the continuing preaching and hearing of the Word in Scripture in the evangelical church catholic.

The Bible does not argue, but assumes, the interaction with human purposes of a purpose more tenacious, more patient than the sense of destiny of any people or civilization. The possibility of such an interaction is precisely what we should like to argue, yet the Bible haunts us. However deeply we bury the awareness in our subconscious minds, we know that we are seen, and judged, and we know it because the writers of the Bible knew it first. Ideas about God we can juggle more or less expertly, but the unpredictable, the actual, the living God is the skeleton that will not rest silently in the closet. At the moment, perhaps, the Bible is too little read or preached, and consequently the will and activity of God in our immediate crises are most imperfectly discerned.

Presently, however, as so often before, the Bible will again be waited on in the listening congregation as the prompting script of God's dialogue with *this* generation, and presently God's intention will be known and obeyed.

CHAPTER SEVEN

Ethics and Politics

WE HAVE COMMENTED on the ultimate source and authority of evangelical faith, the evangelical conception of the way of salvation, and the nature of the evangelical church and Bible. We may now consider certain characteristically Protestant views of Christian life and conduct.

For a first generalization, it may be said that Protestantism rejected the double standard in Christian ethics which had been prevalent since Constantine, and once again laid on the consciences of all Christians the full gospel requirement of perfection.

The Protestant "Vocation"

Evangelical perfection, it will be recalled, was, from the days of Constantine, the aspiration only of the monk. The monkish life was consequently referred to as "the religious" life, and the word "vocation," or "calling," was restricted to this way of life, which of all ways of life was particularly called and dedicated to God. All other activities of society were, from the religious point of view, just ways of earning a living.

Now came Brother Martin, who had been an exemplary monk for decades, to say that all these values of the monastic life were available to any believer who would go about his regular legitimate business with the dedication and religious spirit of monasticism at its best. Every legitimate activity could become a "vocation" if undertaken as a means of serving God, and as we have previously observed, could become a highly effective form of "preaching" the gospel to others engaged in the same activity.

The conception of a Christian vocation was conceived in Lutheranism in too passive a sense to be widely effective in transforming society. Luther was socially conservative and thought still in terms of agrarian society with its class divisions of peasants and landlords. A vocation for him was largely a matter of accepting one's appointed station and its attendant duties and hardships with joyful submission. The only social relationships which Lutheranism actively sought to penetrate with the new spirit of the gospel were those of the family. In our twentieth century disintegration of family life, it is well for us to remember the profound effect Protestantism has had on civilization for four hundred years by making the family a religious as well as biological and economic community. Those who admire ecclesiastical virginity for its own sake have never been able to forgive Luther's marriage to the ex-nun Katherine. This was not, despite vulgar polemics, another case of Henry VIII and Anne Boleyn, but the result of Luther's tardy conviction that his preaching about the Christian dignity of the married estate would gain force by demonstration. Neither lust nor modern romantic love played a role here, but something deeper than either, the service of God in the role of spouse and parent. Protestantism has discovered that both the prayer and the self-mortification of the monastery can readily permeate family relations and in the mutual ministry of this intimate fellowship in labor and in family worship much of the secret of Protestant strength has lain. Protestantism has also known its celibates "for the sake of the Kingdom," but honors them only for that reason.

It was Calvinism which interpreted the doctrine of vocation in an activist sense, justifying the change of business and of social status, if done not for greed or ambition but for a more ample obedience.

These Protestant "vocations in the world" became the means of the greatest penetration of Christianity into culture which the history of the faith has seen. This was to be a regulation of political and economic and social and cultural life, no longer by the occasional external intervention of the clerical hierarchy, but from *within*, by the dedicated consciences of Protestant monks-in-the-world. This was the work primarily of the Calvinist-influenced churches of France, Switzerland, Holland, England, Scotland, and New England, and while it lasted at full strength only about three generations, to the middle or end of the seventeenth century, its impact on the enduring life and institutions of all these countries has been immeasurable. These churches possess a recognizable unity of ethos in their inheritance of a keen

113

interest in politics, but not for the sake of the state, active industry within the economic sphere, but not for the sake of wealth, unceasing labor, ever disciplining the senses, and all originally to glorify God, to produce the Holy Community.

We are still living in the backwash of this mightiest attempt of Christianity to make the kingdoms of this world confess the Kingdom of God, and while the forms of this Calvinist and Puritan discipline are not much more applicable than the medieval pattern Rome is still recommending for the present crisis in Western civilization, nevertheless the memory of these attempts should give us courage and guidance.

Puritan Political Ethics

Noting the sharp contrast with the patriarchal Lutheran tradition of the Continent, we may properly dwell at more length on the most influential political ethic of the modern world, the Puritan democracy of the English-speaking countries. Liberalism, both in terms of civil liberties and of popular participation in government, was in considerable degree shaped if not created by the Puri-

114

tans of England and America. To this day Anglo-American liberalism, even in its secularized forms, shows a humanitarian, responsible and freedom-loving aspect little evident in the liberalism of Romanist and Lutheran countries. Liberalism in Holland, England and North America has been significantly Christianized. In Romanist France, Italy, Spain, Latin America, as in Orthodox Russia and Lutheran Germany, political, religious and intellectual liberty has only been won, where it has been won, by co-operation with antireligious forces against the intolerance and authoritarianism of the clergy. The single most important factor in this contrast is the unique capacity of the Puritan tradition to meet and to mold in Christian forms the aspiration of the modern nations for intellectual and political freedom.

We may begin with the issue of civil liberties and the separation of church and state and then proceed to the topic of responsible general participation in the democratic process. The unique relationship of church and state in this country, and our conception of religious liberty, are a legacy from Puritanism in the free-church phase. In contrast to all the authoritarian church-state systems, Puritanism was gradually persuaded that the freedom of the church from state control, and of the state from ecclesiastical control, was healthy, provided community and state still felt themselves obligated to the fundamental moralities of Christianity. Such a mutual recognition of authority and responsibility on the part of the administrators of church and state is the first condition of religious liberty and its consequences, civil liberties in general.

Modern Romanism, however, has no use for religious and civil liberty. The papacy, moreover, does not feel wholly free to accomplish its mission until it actually governs governments. This is not true, of course, of the great majority of American Catholic laity, who like the dubiously orthodox Al Smith, are willing to fight for the emancipation of their church, but not for that fuller "freedom" which means servitude and sullen silence for non-Romanists. This they learned, however, not from Rome but from their Protestant neighbors. Rome repudiates freedom of conscience and religion and seeks to muzzle all others while gaining for itself legal and financial establishment by the state. Under a Catholic adjustment of the Constitution, private worship would be assured to all groups which should loom no larger than "an insignificant and ostracized sect." But free speech in pulpit and press and exemption from taxation would be denied them, for "error has not the same rights as truth." These proposals are conceded to be "intolerant, but not therefore unreasonable."* Wherever the hierarchy gains influence, however, in the schools, in the courts, in municipal politics, in diplomacy and the state department, in control of the means of communication, this is its program.

The second aspect of Puritan political ethics, popular participation in the democratic process, is more elusive. It is apparent enough, on the face of it, that the democratic process as understood in America is simply a social and political application of the dynamic Protestant conception of the church as the mutual ministry of believers. It is equally

* Ryan and Boland, *Catholic Principles of Politics* (New York: The Macmillan Company, 1940), pp. 313-321.

117

apparent that the whole structure of our government is a political equivalent of the Calvinist and conciliarist pattern of a graduated system of representative legislative bodies. Having observed these striking parallels, however, it is much more difficult to establish the actual relations between the spirit and form of church and state, either historically or in present practice.

The evidence seems, however, to warrant some confidence that there is a significant carry-over from the religious to the political community. This was more evident in the Reformation epoch and the generations immediately following than it is now, for then the various "secular" aspects of life were more vividly measured by the standards of Christian obedience than is now the case. Sunday by Sunday and every day between, it was laid on the consciences of individual members of the Calvinist and Puritan tradition that they were personally responsible for the political conduct of the states of which they were citizens. This is a very different teaching from the paternalism enjoined by ecclesiastically minded Romanists, Anglicans, Lutherans and Orthodox. There it was a matter of submission to the duly constituted authorities, never of personal responsibility for the ethical character of their policies. Romanists, to be sure, were willing to urge resistance to political absolutism, but only in the name and under orders of Roman absolutism. No other religious tradition has systematically trained whole peoples to a sense of their individual and inalienable moral responsibility for the acts of their government.

The mutuality, the tolerance and trust, the give and take of the democratic process is similarly related to the life of the Protestant religious fellowship. It is the democratic conviction that policy is best determined by the conversation and debate of all the several constituent members of the community, each forming and changing his judgment freely and responsibly in the light of his moral obligations. The balance and efficiency of this process are impeded in proportion as members of the political community are denied this responsible participation, as in the case of members of the Communist party, or Roman Catholics. In political decisions of various types, more comprehensive for Communists than for Romanists, their followers are denied freedom of discussion or decision and sent to vote under orders. On a wide range of issues, such as educational policy on local, state, and national levels, questions of social health and morals involved in birth control, marriage and divorce legislation, questions of the immunity of the Roman clergy and property from civil law, and many issues of foreign policy, the Roman Catholic citizen withdraws from the democratic process. His vote is cast under penalty of church discipline by politicians of the hierarchy who do not submit their purposes or criteria to public discussion. These policies naturally ramify out into alliances with specific political machines, or punitive measures against specific independent legislators, and the last implications may be remote indeed. Educated Romanists, to be sure, tend to treasure the independence of their political decisions, but the masses perforce take the priests' opinion as to when Roman morals or interests are involved in political questions.

Now American Roman Catholics have proved their loyalty to this country in all her wars. They have not been demonstrated to be more susceptible to political corruption than non-Catholics, other factors being equal. One may, nevertheless, doubt whether they will or can contribute their proportionate share to American democracy. Roman Catholic democrats are concerned about this weakness, but the cause lies in the very heart of the system. An absolutism can train solid, loyal, efficient, law-abiding citizens, but it cannot train them to be *free;* it cannot produce responsible initiative in each individual layman. Romanism could never have created the Anglo-Saxon type of democracy and it is unlikely to contribute its share toward its maintenance.

Yet the heirs of the Puritans have no grounds for complacency. Much of the history of the last two hundred and fifty years has been a record of the increasing retrenchment and impoverishment of the Protestant ethic. Business and politics in particular were very widely declared out of bounds for the Christian conscience, and the Christian was recommended to "save his soul" as an individual and to be "religious" in one carefully insulated department of his mind and heart. Thus Protestantism has notably regressed to the medieval conception of "the religious" life as a segregated life of pietistic emotion and thought. The tide is unmistakably turning, to be sure, but the recovery of an evangelical ethic will be an arduous struggle. Everywhere over the Protestant world, however, there are springing to light little groups and communities of those quickened by the eternal gospel and determined to build a new fellowship with an ethic related to every aspect of life in society. Protestantism is in revolution because the evangelical movement is again on the march.

The Motive and Hope of Christians

In a deeper sense than Bossuet understood, revolution is the proper state for the evangelical community. The Protestant vocation can never finally be defined in terms of any institution or program, monarchical, parliamentary, capitalistic, socialistic, although every generation must make its responsible decisions for some such structure and Protestants have championed all these. Nor will Protestantism ever rival the ecclesiastical machinery and bureaucracy of the sacrosanct institutions. The role of the Protestant institution is to preserve the gospel which calls every institution to judgment, and the Protestant church has done its duty if it has brought down on itself the truly evangelical criticism of its children. In a day of insecurity and widespread yearning for authority, Protestantism is no doubt at some disadvantage. Yet if Protestantism is defensive about its established position and practices, it becomes an *ersatz* Catholicism and loses its reason for existence. Protestantism can save its life only by losing it. All securities and institutions must be relinquished before the one security, the will of the living God speaking through the mutual ministry of believers. As Richard Niebuhr wrote of the Puritans who came to New England, "What they did not foresee was that the positive part of church reformation was not a structure, but a life, a movement, which could never come to rest again in secure habitations, but needed to go on and on from camp to camp to its meeting with the evercoming Kingdom."

Like the Marxist, the Christian knows of a power at work in history independent of his desires or even his existence, but to which he may become associated, and in which he may find his fulfillment. Unlike the Marxist, however, the Christian may commune directly with this power, and discover in it a solicitation for himself apart from his role as a unit in class and national struggles. The most orthodox socialist, democrat, capitalist or pacifist may also be personally unstable and antisocial and none of these programs answers the ultimate problem of individual life. For the short term such political religions seem more effective than Christianity, which can never seem to state clearly and simply whether it is socialist, capitalist, pacifist, democratic. And just for that reason the political religion must be ruthless. As the Marxist said to the Christian, "We are more desperate than you, for we have but this once. If we fail now, we fail forever. You can fail and fail and yet succeed."

The bond of Christian fellowship cuts deeper and lasts longer than any ethical program because it assumes the inadequacy and evil in every ethical program in which Christians are engaged. Christian soldiers can even fight each other with a deep sense of fellowship, as lovers forgive in each other their mutual exploitation or as parents and children, employers and employees perceive and forgive in each other their lust to domination and self-assertion. For Christians have a hope which cannot be dashed by the perishing of any specific state or civilization or reform. In a time of the breaking of nations it is hard to see what other hope than this can endure, save the hope of death and oblivion. The Christian expects something less than social or political or economic success, and something vastly more, a fulfillment and transfiguration of his fragmentary and halting obedience in the life of God himself. Yet this resurrection and transfiguration will be of the "body," that is, of the concrete personality in all its social and historical relations.

The Christian's hope is thus implicit in his first confession before the figure of Jesus Christ: "My Lord and my God!" The recognition that in Jesus Christ there is more than superlative goodness, that there is also ultimate *power,* is at the same time the recognition that the destroyer and creator of nature, the exuberant energies of the universe, are ultimately Christlike, and *good.* The God of nature is not in the last analysis as D. H. Lawrence or Robinson Jeffers sees him, beautiful and cruel and careless, but the Father of our Lord Jesus Christ. Thus it is first from our redemption that we understand the creation and our place in the world of things. God has scattered hints of himself everywhere, in "the starry sky above and the moral law within," and has permitted man the means of an imposing accumulation of useful science, but for a certain and saving knowledge of the significance of our lives and their proper orientation we must turn to the particular revelation in history of Jesus his Messiah. As our personal decisions are shaped in personal relations with the community of believers and Christ its head, so we perceive these qualities and relations to be the most determinative factors in the universe, the crucial revelatory moments of the intention and meaning of the whole continuous creative process of the cosmos. In the degree that the Christian puts his faith in Christ, he dares to trust the unknown God. He is assured that although many of God's ways will remain incomprehensible to him, nevertheless, in Christ he has the full and adequate presentation of God's nature and purpose so far as mortality is capable of it.

We may feel, with Luther, that the "Trinity" is an inappropriately mathematical term for God but we discover its essential meaning implicit in the good news of the historical revelation. We know that no spirit is the Holy Spirit which is not also the Spirit of Jesus Christ, and we know that all we can comprehend of the hidden Father is fully disclosed in Jesus Christ. And knowing that the Eternal bears Jesus Christ risen in glory in his unending life we can dare to hope also for everlasting life in him. Thus it is that to the three major ventures of the church's oldest confession of faith is added the audacious Christian hope:

> I believe in God the Father Almighty, maker of heaven and earth, . . .
> > and in Jesus Christ, his only son, our Lord . . .
> > in the Holy Spirit, the holy church catholic, the communion of saints, the forgiveness of sins, . . .
> > the resurrection of the body, and the life everlasting. Amen.